# the story of...

# ANNE FRANK

Author
Jim Pipe

# THE CAST

**Anne Frank:** *Born in 1929, Anne (Annelies Marie) Frank was a German-Jewish teenager who was forced to go into hiding during World War II/the Holocaust. After being betrayed, Anne and her family were arrested and sent to a Nazi concentration camp. In March 1945, she died at Bergen-Belsen camp, aged just 15. While in hiding, this brave, bright and lively girl wrote a diary, which has become one of most widely read books in the world.*

**Otto Frank:** *After serving in the German Army during World War I, Anne's father Otto worked in a bank. Following Hitler's rise to power in 1933, he started a new business in Amsterdam. It was above this office that the Frank family hid during the war. Modest, kind and resourceful, Mr Frank was a tower of strength in the flat – tutoring Anne and her sister and calming everyone's nerves during moments of crisis. The only member of the secret flat to survive the war, Otto published Anne's diary in 1947.*

**Margot Frank:** *Three years older than Anne, Margot was considered the more beautiful and the more intelligent of the two sisters, which Anne naturally resented at times. However, during the two years that they were confined in the flat, the two sisters eventually became close friends. After the group was sent to concentration camps, Anne and Margot managed to remain together until almost the end. Like Anne, Margot died of typhus at Bergen-Belsen camp some time in March 1945.*

**Edith Frank:** *Born in 1900, Anne's mother Edith Hollander was the daughter of a manufacturer. She grew up in the town of Aachen but moved to Frankfurt after marrying Otto in 1925. Edith was used to living in a big house with servants so she found life in the secret flat very difficult – perhaps one reason she and Anne did not always get on well. Edith died from hunger at Auschwitz in Janaury 1945, just 10 days before the guards fled the camp.*

**Peter van Pels:** *The son of Hermann van Pels, who went into business with Otto Frank in 1938. Peter's family fled from Germany the previous year and moved into the secret flat a week after the Frank family. A simple but kind boy, Peter was sometimes teased by Anne. But as time passed, Anne gradually became closer and closer to Peter, eventually falling in love with him. The pair were seperated at Auschwitz and Peter died a few months later on a forced march in freezing conditions.*

**Miep Gies:** *Miep was among the staff of Otto Frank's Opekta company in Amsterdam who helped the Frank and van Pels families to hide during the war. Miep brought them food and news from the outside. She organised gifts and surprises on birthdays and festivals and did what she could to make life better for the hidden families. It was Miep who found and hid Anne Franks diary after the family's arrest, which she later gave to Otto.*

Copyright © ticktock Entertainment Ltd. 2006
First published in Great Britain in 2006 by ticktock Media Ltd.,
Unit 2, Orchard Business Centre, North Farm Road, Tunbridge Wells, Kent, TN2 3XF
ISBN 1 84696 001 0
Printed in China
A CIP catalogue record for this book is available from the British Library.

# CONTENTS

# THE RISE OF THE NAZIS

In 1918 the world had been at war for over three years. Over 15 million soldiers and civilians had died and Europe was turned into a giant battlefield. But by the summer of 1918, the Allies – France, the US and Britain – were slowly pushing forwards.

By November, the Germans had surrendered. At the Treaty of Versailles, the Allies forced Germany to pay them huge sums of money, called reparations. Germany also lost territory.

In the first few years after the war, life was hard. But by the mid-1920s many people were better off and could enjoy life.

Why are these people so happy? We lost the war.

Let's get out of here.

We could have won. Now look at Germany.

Our lousy politicians stabbed us in the back.

Many German ex-soldiers were still angry about losing the war. They blamed the new government for the Treaty of Versailles.

One of these bitter ex-soldiers, Adolf Hitler, set up a new party, the National Socialists, or Nazis.

People are angry and afraid. I can use that to help us get into power.

Hitler was a brilliant speaker. He persuaded thousands of ex-soldiers to join the Nazis.

In November 1923, Hitler tried to start a revolt in Munich, but it was quickly put down by the army.

I'm desperate. What can I do?

There are no jobs in Germany now.

Our money is worth nothing any more.

Hitler was sent to prison for 9 months. This gave him time to think about how to gain power, and it was while he was in prison that he wrote a book about his plan, Mein Kampf (My Struggle). At first, the Nazis weren't very popular. Then, in 1929, the German economy collapsed. Many workers lost their jobs and their savings.

More and more people hoped that Hitler would make Germany strong again. He blamed the Jews for all their problems, and many Germans were happy to believe him.

People will vote me into power.

The Jews are stealing your jobs and your money. It's time to fight back!

You're right! It's all their fault.

APPLAUSE!

Hitler's private army, the "stormtroops", began to attack Jewish shops and buildings.

SMASH!

Go back to where you came from!

Take that, you dirty Jews!

This was the world that Anne Frank grew up in, where simply being Jewish could lead to attack, imprisonment and murder...

FAST FACT  The Nazi swastika designed by Hitler was based on an ancient symbol that has been in use for over 3,000 years. It originally stood for life and goodness.

7

# ANNE FRANK'S EARLY YEARS

Anne Frank was born on June 12, 1929. She was the second daughter of Otto and Edith Frank, who were German Jews. The Franks lived in Frankfurt, Germany. Members of their family had lived there for 300 years.

Margot, meet your new sister Anne!

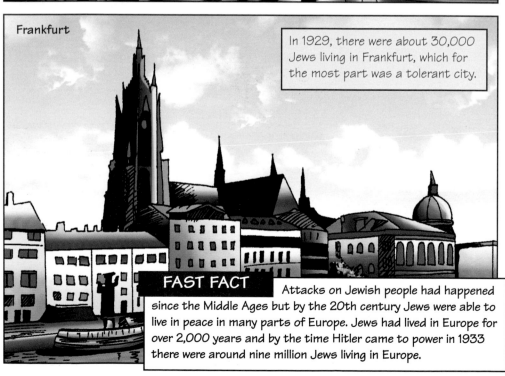

Frankfurt

In 1929, there were about 30,000 Jews living in Frankfurt, which for the most part was a tolerant city.

**FAST FACT** Attacks on Jewish people had happened since the Middle Ages but by the 20th century Jews were able to live in peace in many parts of Europe. Jews had lived in Europe for over 2,000 years and by the time Hitler came to power in 1933 there were around nine million Jews living in Europe.

Like many Jews, Anne's father Otto had fought for the German Army during World War I.

Otto's brother Robert          Otto

After the war, Otto worked in his father's bank. At this time, he met Anne's mother Edith.

Edith, you look lovely today!

Otto and Edith married in 1925.

The Franks had a happy family life in Frankfurt.

Anne, we need to get you some new shoes.

Can I play with my friends when I get home?

Soon the Franks started to fear for their future in Germany.

We won't be safe with Hitler in Power.

THE JEWS are our enemy!

Listen to that!

In January 1933, Adolf Hitler was made German Chancellor. The Nazis were finally in power.

HEIL HITLER!

Hitler soon showed he meant business. Jews lost their jobs and their stores were boycotted. Jewish books were burned.

Jude!

The Nazis want Jewish people to leave Germany.

Why are they picking on us?

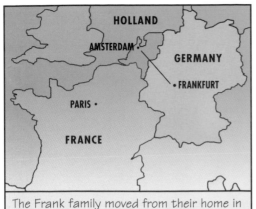

The Frank family moved from their home in Germany to Amsterdam in Holland.

The Franks decided to leave Germany.

We can be safe in Amsterdam.

In the summer of 1933, Otto Frank left for Holland.

In Amsterdam, Otto worked hard to set up a new business, the Dutch Opekta Company. He sold pectin, a powder used to make jam and gravy.

Welcome to your new home! I think you'll like it here.

Father!!

Less than a year later, Edith, Margot and Anne, (now four years old) joined Otto in Amsterdam.

Anne enjoyed her first years in Amsterdam. By the mid-1930s the Franks had settled into a normal routine in their new apartment at 37 Merwedeplei.

Those tulips are beautiful.

We'll miss you father!

Catch me if you can, Anne!

You're too fast Margot!

Come and play with us Anne!

Anne and Margot went to a Montessori school and made lots of new friends.

Say hello to Anne everyone!

They spent their holidays at the seaside.

Otto's business was going well. In 1938, Hermann van Pels becomes his business partner.

It's a deal.

But the hatred the Franks had tried to leave behind followed them.

I can't believe it! How can the Nazis get away with it?

Back in Germany, many synagogues and thousands of Jewish shops had been smashed and burned by Nazi stormtroops.

Germany is for Germans, not Jews!

Smash them all!

## FAST FACT

On November 9 and 10th 1938, the Nazis destroyed over 7,000 Jewish shops all over Germany, and attacked 267 synagogues. Because of all the broken windows, this event became known as Kristallnacht (the Night of Broken Glass).

In November 1938, the Nazis began the first mass arrests of Jews. 30,000 men and boys were sent to concentration camps.

Get a move on!

By 1939, half of the Jews living in Germany had fled, including Anne's uncles, who went to America.

Anne's grandmother went to live with them in Amsterdam.

Welcome to Amsterdam Granny!

Then, in September 1939, Hitler invaded Poland. World War II had begun.

# LIFE UNDER THE NAZIS

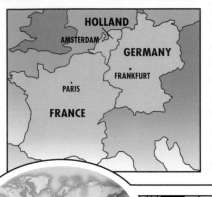

In May 1940, the Germans invaded Holland and France. The Franks were once again forced to live under Nazi rule. There was no escape - Nazi soldiers guarded the train stations and borders. Every Dutch citizen was forced to carry an Identification (ID) card. This made it easy for the Germans to know who was Jewish and where they lived.

Is the war over then?

Not for us. The Nazis hate the Jews.

Well, I hate the Nazis. What have we ever done to them?

Sshhh. Keep your voice down Anne!

From now on, we have to be very careful what we say.

The Germans introduced ration books. you could not buy food from a shop without them.

I'd like some sugar and flour please.

At first, Anne and Margot's lives didn't change much. They could still play with their friends and went to school. But soon everything was to change...

The Germans, helped by Dutch Nazis, created laws against the Jews as they had in Germany. They forced Jews to hand over their businesses to non-Jews. Otto had expected this. He had already signed his business over to his non-Jewish colleagues Victor Kugler and Johannes Kleiman.

I'll put the business in your names.

You can trust us, You're still the boss.

In February 1941 the Dutch Nazis raided Jewish markets. Many Jews fought back. But German soldiers were called in and over 400 Jewish men and boys were rounded up.

Did you hear about the arrests?

Nobody knows where they have been taken.

From now on, Jews in the Netherlands were in real danger.

**FAST FACT** The Dutch Nazis worked with the Germans. Some are paid informers who spied on Jews. The penalty for sheltering a Jew was extremely severe. Anyone guilty of this 'crime' could be taken away and shot immediately, or thrown into prison by the Nazi authorities.

Soon Jews were not allowed in cinemas or parks, or to ride in cars and trains.

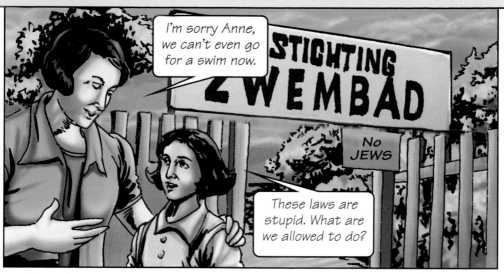

I'm sorry Anne, we can't even go for a swim now.

STICHTING ZWEMBAD

No JEWS

These laws are stupid. What are we allowed to do?

You're going to have to go to a new school, too.

That's not fair... I'm not going.

It's the law Anne. Jews can't go to Dutch schools anymore.

Anne soon settled into the Jewish school. She became good friends with Peter Wessel, who cycled home with her.

Hurry up slowcoach!

Your long black hair makes you look like a wild pony Anne!

The winter of 1941-42 was long and hard.

Soon after Christmas, Anne's Granny fell ill and died.

With all that's going on, maybe your Granny is the lucky one.

The laws became stricter. Jews had to wear a yellow star.

### FAST FACT

From April 1942, Jews in Holland had to wear the yellow Star of David, bearing the word JOOD (Jew) on their clothes.

Jews were not allowed out after 8 pm.

Don't be late!

Anne did her best to enjoy the summer. She hung out friends playing table tennis and eating ice-cream.

It's delicious!

The Nazis are killing Jews in the camps.

We've got to go into hiding, before it's too late.

Then the Germans began to arrest Jews just for being Jews.

Where can we hide?

There are rooms above my office.

Otto asks his partner Mr Van Pels to join him.

How can we ever thank you?

There is room for both our families.

The hiding place is a secret flat on the top two floors of Otto's office at 263 Prinsengracht.

Otto's office staff agree to help. These friends and employees kept the business operating and risked their lives to help the Frank family survive.

Victor Kugler

Otto

Jo Kleiman

Bep Voskuijl

Miep Gies

Jan Gies

# INTO HIDING!

For months, the Franks and their helpers moved their furniture bit by bit into the secret flat. They stored food supplies in the attic.

Watch your back!

Phew! These bags of flour are heavy.

The plans were going well. Then one day, a policeman knocked on the door with a letter for Margot.

Margot was terrified.

The Nazis are sending me to a work camp.

They'll kill you!

No! They can't take you away.

There's no time to lose. We going into hiding.

Anne packed her bag with books and photos.

Memories mean more to me than dresses.

Otto alerts the Opekta staff.

Miep, we've got to move fast.

The next day, July 6th, Anne wakes up at 5.30am. The Franks get ready to move.

Stuff that into my pocket.

Wear as much as you can dear.

I feel like I'm going to the North Pole!

## FAST FACT

The Franks could not be seen carrying suitcases - it would give their plan away. Instead, Anne put on two vests, three pairs of pants, a dress, a skirt, a jacket and a raincoat. These were her only possessions that she took with her to her new home.

Margot rode ahead with Miep.

Anne walked with her parents. The Franks left notes pretending that thy had escaped abroad.

Goodbye Moortie!

Hermann

Auguste

Peter

A week later, on July 13, the van Pels family joined the Franks. Anne Frank's family and the other residents of the secret flat were in hiding for two years. The flat was cramped and they had to be very careful not to be seen or heard. For two years, they lived in fear of a knock on the door...

The secret flat was on two floors, though the Franks and Van Pels families also used the office rooms on the 1st floor at weekends and in the evenings,

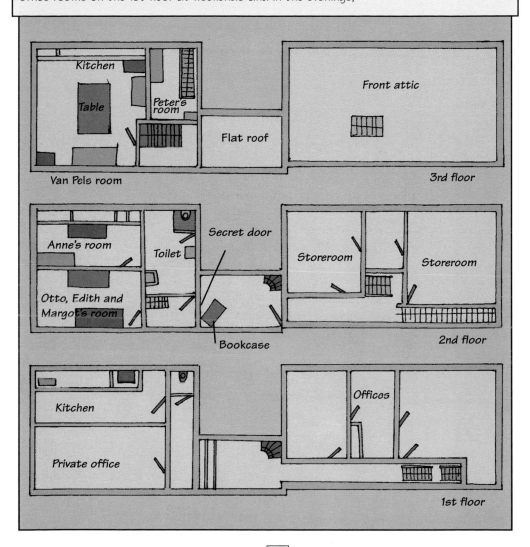

Kitchen

Table

Peter's room

Front attic

Flat roof

Van Pels room

3rd floor

Anne's room

Toilet

Secret door

Storeroom

Storeroom

Otto, Edith and Margot's room

Bookcase

2nd floor

Kitchen

Offices

Private office

1st floor

Anne got her diary as a present on her 13th birthday, just two weeks before she went into hiding.

Anne kept a diary of her life. Up in the attic, she wrote down her experiences of life in hiding.

*Peter van Pels is so boring!*

Anne shared her secrets with her diary.

*Why does everyone always pick on me?*

*your DIARIES ARE IMPORTANT*

*I've always wanted to be a writer, I'll write my diaries like a novel.*

When Anne heard on the radio her diary might be published, she changed the names of the people in the flat. So the van Pels family are called van Daan in her diary.

## FAST FACT

Anne received her diary as a 13th birthday present. She wrote her diary in the form of letters addressed to "Kitty".

One of the first jobs is to cover up the windows,

These curtains may not look much but they could save our lives.

They listen to English radio each night.

*This is* **London** *Calling*

**Ssshh.** Turn it down. Someone might hear us.

Let's hope there is good news.

They work for Opekta making jams from fruit and filling gravy packets.

This will keep us busy.

We should get some games too.

SUG

Mr Kugler got a trustworthy carpenter to build a bookcase in front of the entrance to the flat.

This will open like a door. Now the flat is truly secret!

Miep Gies and Bep Voskuijl secretly brought food to the flat.

Ration books could be bought illegally on the black market, but they were very expensive.

Anne found it hard being cooped up inside the flat.

Sobbing

Everything has gone wrong. I should be outside, playing with my friends.

Life was either very boring - or terrifying!

What's that noise? It sounded like footsteps!

Anne did not always get on with the others in the flat.

You're so bossy Mrs van Pels.

And you're just a rude little girl.

She tried to study every day, but it was hard without a teacher.

Yawn! This is so boring.

Everyone took turns to wash themselves in a tin tub.

Careful Margot - don't let anyone see you.

Anne could never forget the danger. When a plumber came to fix the pipes, they had to sit still for three days.

It's too noisy to use the toilet.

We'll have to use this basin instead.

Margot...

Sssh. If you have to speak, whisper!

At night the girls did stretching exercises to keep themselves fit,

CREAK!

Ice Skates! Just what I wanted...

To pass the time, Anne imagined shopping in Switzerland with her cousin Bernd.

# A NEW OCCUPANT

On 16 November, 1942, the seven Jews in the flat were joined by an eighth, Fritz Pfeffer. He was shocked to see them.

Everyone thought you had escaped to Belgium.

Join us! Have some coffee and cognac!

Mr Pfeffer explained how their Jewish friends had been taken away by the Gestapo.

No one is spared. The sick, the young and the elderly are all marched to their death.

The Gestapo were the Nazi secret police. They prowled the streets at night looking for Jews and offered bribes to anyone who had information about them.

My god! Those rats are huge - and they're eating our supplies!

GASP!

At times being trapped in the flat was a nightmare. Amsterdam was bombed by Allied planes and anti-aircraft guns kept them awake all night. Then Peter discovered a swarm of rats in the attic.

SCUTTLE

But there were good days. The Opekta staff gave everyone a gift on St Nicholas' Day (5 December).

Happy St Nicholas Day everybody!

Do stop wriggling Mrs van Pels.

AARGH!

Mr Pfeffer, a dentist, pulled out two of Mrs van Pels teeth, much to everyone's amusement!

Youch! That looks painful.

Meanwhile, as the months passed, Anne grew closer and closer to Peter van Pels.

It really helps to talk to you.

It helps me too. I used to think you were so shy!

I think I'm falling in love. What would it be like to kiss him?

They found it hard to spend time alone.

I wish we could talk but everyone if watching.

Finally, they kissed!

But Otto did not approve.

Be careful Anne, don't take it too seriously!

The Franks had been in the flat for 18 months. But now there was real hope. The Nazis were in retreat everywhere.

By the beginning of 1944, all the flat could think about is an Allied invasion of France - and freedom!

Do you think we could be free soon?

We have to be patient.

But life was getting tougher by the day. The flat was short of food, soap and clothes.

You know that's all we have left.

Yuck! I'm sick of spinach and potatoes.

Burglars started to break into office storerooms, hoping to find food and supplies.

I pray its not the Gestapo?

Then one night...

CRASH!

Quick, I heard a noise downstairs.

Be careful, we don't know who it is.

Burglars had broken in to the storeroom, but Mr van Pels scared them off.

HALT! Police!

A few minutes later, a bright light shone into the room. Was it the Gestapo? The members of the flat rushed back upstairs.

RUN!

"We're too late. It looks like the burglars have scarpered."

Later, the Dutch police searched the building. They even walked up to the bookcase, rattled it — but found nothing,

Upstairs, the members of the flat sat in the dark, shivering with fear. But they had escaped again.

Everyone was very shaken by the break in. But two months later, there was fantastic news. The Americans and British had landed in France.

Then news arrived of an attempt on Hitler's life. He survived, but freedom seemed closer than ever.

"By October I could be back in school!"

# THE FINAL MONTHS

Then, at around 10 o' clock in the morning, August 4, 1944, the Frank family's greatest fear came true. Victor Kugler heard a knock on the door to the office. Suddenly, a group of men led by a Nazi officer burst in.

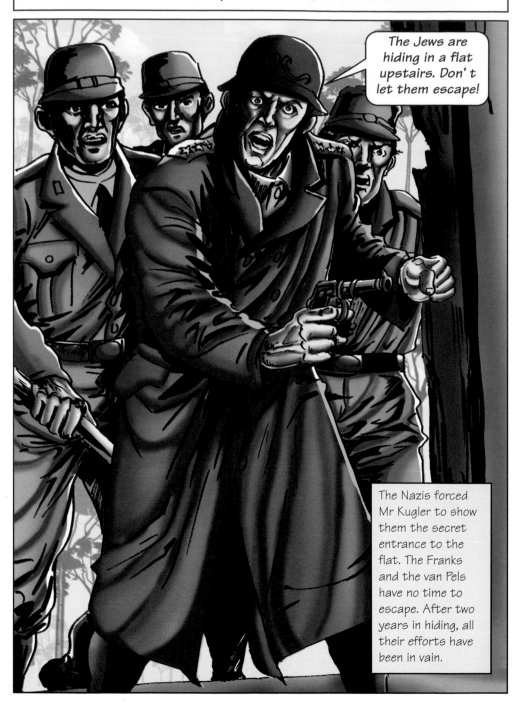

Hand over your cash and valuables.

Take them away. Their holiday is over!

Anne and the other terrified members of the flat were led down the stairs and pushed into a waiting truck.

Shut up and get in!

Where are they taking us?

Victor Kugler and Jo Kleiman were also arrested by the police.

But Miep was not arrested. She later found the scattered pages of Anne's diary in the flat.

The Franks and the van Pels families were taken to Westerbork camp in the north of the Netherlands. Then, on September 3rd 1944, they were put on a train to the infamous death camp, Auschwitz, in Poland.

If we get separated, look after each other my darlings.

The Nazis packed Jews onto trains like cattle. The journey took three days and many people died on the way.

At the death camp, Jews were divided into two groups - those who would work, and those who would die.

Hey you! Get into this line.

As the Nazis retreated from the Russians, Margot and Anne were moved back to Germany to another camp, Belsen.

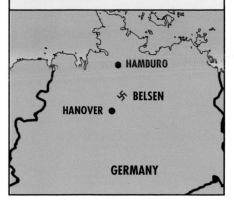

Belsen is dirty and ridden with disease.

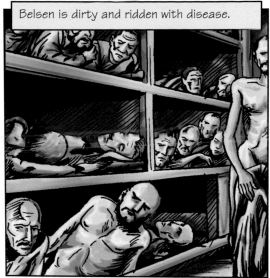

In March 1945, just weeks before their camp was liberated (freed) by the British soldiers, Anne and Margot got sick with typhus. Weakened by starvation, they soon died. Anne was just 15 years old.

## FAST FACT

In all, over 6 million Jews were murdered by the Nazis. One and a half million victims were children. Death camps such as Auschwitz were giant factories of death, gassing thousands of people to death each day.

On May 8th, 1945 the war in Europe ended. Allied troops were horrified by what they found at the camps - terrible scenes of death, disease and starvation.

Otto Frank is the only survivor of th eight who hid in the flat. In 1953, he marries another survivor of Auschwitz, Elfriede Markovits. He dies in Switzerland in 1980, aged 91.

All the Opekta helpers survived the war. Victor Kugler escaped from a Dutch prison camp and Jo Kleiman was released because of his poor health.

Otto was given Anne's diary pages by Miep Gies, and in 1947 published them in her memory. Today over 30 million copies have been sold.

The house with the secret flat at 263 Prinsengracht is now a museum.

A memorial to Anne and Margot was erected at the site of Belsen camp.

MARGOT FRANK
1926 - 1945
ANNE FRANK
1929 - 1945

Thanks to her diary, Anne's memory and that of other victims of the Nazis will live forever. Her story reminds us of the horrors of war and the terrible price of hatred.

**D**espite being just an ordinary girl from an ordinary family, thanks to her diary, Anne Frank became one of the famous figures of WWII. Her move to Holland and into hiding typified the terror many Jews had to face on a daily basis during the Nazi rule, and her tragic death the horror of Hitler's reign.

**1889:** *Otto Frank (Anne's father), is born in Frankfurt, Germany.*

**1900:** *Edith Hollander (Anne's mother), is born in Aachen, Germany.*

**1914-1918:** *World War I. Otto Frank serves in the German Army.*

**1925:** *Otto and Edith Frank marry and settle in Frankfurt, Germany.*

**1926:** *The Franks' first daughter, Margot, is born in Frankfurt am Maim, Germany.*

**June 12, 1929:** *Anneliese Marie, or Anne, is born in Frankfurt, Germany.*

**October 29, 1929:** *Great Depression begins following Wall Street stock market crash.*

**Summer 1933:** *Hitler becomes Chancellor of Germany and creates first anti-Jewish laws.*

**September, 1935:** *- The Nuremberg Laws are passed defining Jews as non-citizens and making mixed Aryan and Jewish marriage illegal.*

**Summer 1937:** *The van Pels family flees from Osnabruck to Holland.*

**November 9-11, 1938:** *Kristallnacht (Night of Broken Glass). Nazis destroy synagogues and Jewish shops across Germany.*

**March, 1939:** *Grandmother Hollander comes to live with the Frank family.*

**Sep 1, 1939:** *World War II begins when Germany invades Poland.*

**May 10, 1940:** *The German army invades the Netherlands.*

**June 12, 1942:** *Anne receives a diary for her 13th birthday.*

**July 5, 1942:** *Margot is ordered to report to labor camp. The Frank family goes into hiding the next day, followed by the van Pels family one week later.*

**November 16, 1942:** *Fritz Pfeffer joins the Frank and van Pels families in the secret flat.*

**August 4, 1944:** *The Franks are arrested, taken to a police station, then to Westerbork, a transit camp in Holland.*

**September 2, 1944:** *Anne and the others in the flat are sent to Auschwitz.*

**October 30, 1944:** *Anne and her sister, Margot, are sent to Bergen-Belsen camp.*

**January 6, 1945:** *Edith Frank dies of starvation in Auschwitz.*

**January 7, 1945:** *Auschwitz is liberated. Otto Frank is the only survivor from the secret flat.*

**March 1945:** *Anne and Margot die of typhus in Bergen-Belsen.*

**May 8, 1945:** *Germany surrenders. World War II ends in Europe.* **Summer 1947:** *Anne's diary is first published, in Dutch (1,500 copies).*

**1** When Hitler first came to power in Germany, he was very popular. He spread his ideas using radio, the press, in films and by speaking at mass meetings. He used his popularity to gain more and more power, banning all opposition parties and sending many opponents to concentration camps.

**2** Like the Franks, many thousands of Jews left Germany in large numbers from 1933 onwards to escape life under the Nazis. But the biggest problem for them was where to go. Many countries set limits on the number of Jews allowed to enter. Some countries even closed their borders and sent ships with Jewish refugees back to Germany.

**3** The Germans used ration cards to control the people of the Netherlands. Any Dutch that broke German laws lost their food. Hiding Jews was punishable by death - one third of the Dutch people who hid Jews did not survive the war.

**4** The Franks had to make a very tough decision about who else to invite to live in the secret flat. They had to rule out the Franks' best friends, the Goslars, because they were afraid their young toddler would make too much noise and give them away.

**5** To set people on the wrong track regarding their whereabouts, the Franks successfully led people to believe that they'd escaped to Switzerland (a neutral country)!

**6** As well as writing her diary Anne Frank also wrote short stories, fairy tales, essays, and the beginnings of a novel during her two years in hiding. Five notebooks and more than 300 loose pages, each written by hand, survived the war, thanks to Miep Gies who rescued them from the secret flat.

**7** When the electricity to the flat was cut off, Anne kept herself amused by spying on her neighbours with a pair of binoculers through a crack in the curtains.

**8** Westerbork was a camp situated in the northeastern Netherlands, near the German border. From 1942 to 1944, the camp served as a transit camp for Jews who were being deported from the Netherlands to eastern Europe.

**9** The Nazis shipped the Jews to concentration camps in rail cars, most of which were cattle cars without windows or heating.

**10** Anne Frank was one of about one million children who died in the Holocaust. Most were sent straight to the gas chambers in concentration camps.

**11** Only 4,700 of the 110,000 Jews deported from the Netherlands to the concentration camps survived. Homecoming was often disappointing - most returning Jews had lost their family and friends. They found their houses occupied and their property stolen.

**12** Anne's diary was first published in Dutch under the title Het Achterhuis, meaning 3The Annexe2. So far it has been published in 70 languages and has sold over 25 million copies.

# GLOSSARY

**Allies:** *A group of 26 nations led by Britain, the United States, and the Soviet Union that fought against Germany, Italy, and Japan (known as the Axis partners) in World War II. In World War I the Allies were a group of nations led by France, Britain, the United States and Russia against Germany, Austro-Hungary and Turkey.*

**Auschwitz-Birkenau:** *The largest Nazi concentration camp, situated in southwest Poland. Over one million Jews were murdered in this camp alone. Anne Frank and the other members of the secret flat were sent to Auschwitz from Westerbork camp in September 1944.*

**Bergen-Belsen:** *A concentration camp in northern Germany. As the Russian army advanced and Jewish camp prisoners were moved from Poland, this camp became more and more overcrowded. More than 34,000 people died in the camp from planned starvation and disease, including Anne and her sister Margot.*

**Black market:** *An illegal market, usually for goods that are in short supply.*

**Great Depression:** *The Great Depression was an economic slump in North America and Europe that began in 1929 and lasted until about 1939. Millions of people around the world lost their jobs and/or their savings.*

**Concentration Camps:** *Prison camps that held Jews, Gypsies and political and religious opponents of the Nazis. In the labour camps, prisoners were forced to work for the Nazis. Six death camps in Poland, including Auschwitz, were built to carry out the mass murder of prisoners.*

**Deportation:** *Forced removal of Jews in Nazi-occupied countries from their homes. Most were shipped to labour or death camps.*

**Dictator:** *A ruler or leader who is unrestrained by law.*

**Gestapo:** *The Secret State Police created by the Nazis to stamp out opposition to Hitler and the Nazi party. They were famous for their brutal methods and were feared across occupied Europe.*

**Holocaust:** *The mass murder of 6 million European Jews by the Nazis.*

**Identification Card:** *A card carrying information about the person who carries it, such as country, religion and address. In Nazi-occupied Netherlands, ID cards had to be carried at all times. ID cards made it very easy for the Nazis to round up Jews and send them to the camps.*

**Informer:** *Someone who reveals confidential information, often in return for money. The Nazis relied on informers to help them hunt down Jews in hiding.*

# GLOSSARY

**Kristallnacht:** *"The Night of Broken Glass", November 9-10, 1938, when the Nazis organised a riot against synagogues, Jewish houses and shops in Germany and Austria. On the same night, 10,000 Jewish men and boys were arrested and sent to concentration camps.*

**Jews:** *A Jew can be someone who practices the Jewish religion, whose mother is Jewish, or is a member of a Jewish community. The Nazis arrested anyone with two or more Jewish grandparents, or anyone married to a Jew.*

**Occupation:** *The control of a country by a foreign military power. Germany occupied the Netherlands and many other European countries during World War II.*

**Nazi:** *A shortened name for the National Socialist party led by Adolf Hitler from 1921 to 1945.*

**Racism:** *The belief that race accounts for differences in human character or ability and that a particular race is superior to others.*

**Rations:** *A way of sharing out food that is in short supply. During World War II, people in many countries were given ration books that contained tokens. These tokens were handed over to shopkeepers to buy foods such as meat, sugar and eggs.*

**Reparations:** *Payment paid after the war by the losers to the winners. After World War I, Germany were forced to pay the Allies for the damage it had caused during the war.*

**Synagogue:** *A building or meeting place for Jewish worship and religious instruction.*

**Stormtroops (Sturmabteilung, or SA):** *These ex-soldiers were used by the Nazis to beat up their political opponents and played a important role in Adolf Hitler©?s rise to power in the 1930s. Stormtroops were often known as brownshirts from the colour of their uniform.*

**Swastika:** *An ancient religious symbol (a hooked cross) that became the official symbol of the Nazi Party with its distinctive red, white and black colours.*

**Treaty of Versailles:** *The peace settlement signed after World War I had ended, which blamed Germany for starting the war and forced her to pay reparations (though Germany ended up paying very little of the total amount).*

**Yellow star:** *The six pointed Star of David was a Jewish symbol that the Nazis forced Jews to wear as a mark of shame and to distinguish them from non-Jews. Anne Frank wore a yellow star from May 1942 until she went into hiding.*

# INDEX